ARTIST
TRANSCRIPTIONS
PIANO

M____Y ALEXANDER
Plays Standards

CONTENTS

Transcribed by Gene Rizzo

Photos courtesy of Telarc Records

ISBN 0-634-03128-7

HAL•LEONARD®
CORPORATION
7777 W. BLUEMOUND RD. P.O. BOX 13819 MILWAUKEE, WI 53213

Visit Hal Leonard Online at
www.halleonard.com

BIOGRAPHY

MONTY ALEXANDER was born in 1944 in Kingston, Jamaica. He began piano lessons at the age of six. As a teenager, he was often invited to sit in with the bands of some of the prominent local musicians. In addition, he had the opportunity to attend performances of Louis Armstrong and Nat "King" Cole at the Carib theatre, and his style of playing was deeply influenced by their "gospel of jazz." He formed a band called Monty and the Cyclones, which recorded songs that charted on the Jamaican pop charts between 1958 and 1960.

He moved to Miami in 1961, and by 1963 was playing piano with Art Mooney's orchestra. Jilly Rizzo and Frank Sinatra heard him, and Monty was hired to play at Jilly's club in New York. There, he played solo and accompanied many well-known personalities of the entertainment world, including Mr. Sinatra. It was at Jilly's that he met vibraharpist Milt Jackson, who hired Monty to join his group. Soon after, Monty began an association with bassist Ray Brown which lasted many years. He also performed with such jazz giants as Dizzy Gillespie, Clark Terry, and Sonny Rollins.

Since 1964, Monty has become extremely active as a pianist and composer. He has recorded with Quincy Jones and was heard on the soundtrack of Clint Eastwood's movie *Bird* about the life of Charlie Parker. In 1991, he assisted Natalie Cole in the seven time grammy award winning album *Unforgettable*, a tribute to her father Nat. In 1993, he performed at Carnegie Hall in a tribute to the beloved pianist Erroll Garner.

From 1993 to 1995, Monty performed at the Montreux Jazz Festival in Switzerlan—two years accompanying opera singer Barbara Hendricks in a program of Duke Ellington compositions, and in 1995 with an all-Jamaican reggae group. This performance was recorded for Island Records, and the CD is called *Yard Movement*. Monty performed Gershwin's *Rhapsody in Blue* with Bobby McFerrin conducting at the Verbier Festival in Switzerland in 1996.

Monty continues to be a much sought-after solo artist and accompanist, with over fifty CDs released under his own name. He presents music in several contexts: soloist, trio format, performances with big band or symphony orchestra, and a return to his Jamaican roots with the unique "groovin'" jazz-reggae sounds heard on several recent albums on the Concord and Island labels.

Body and Soul

Words by Edward Heyman, Robert Sour and Frank Eyton
Music by John Green

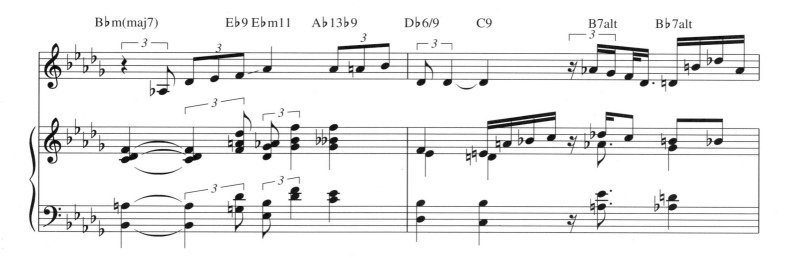

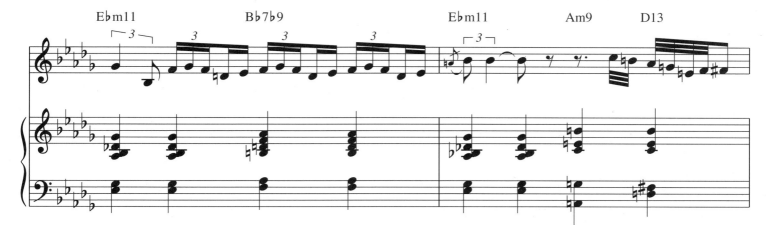

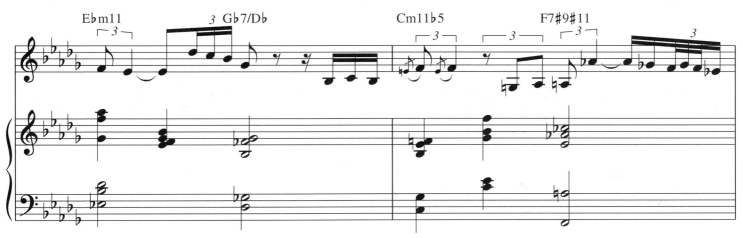

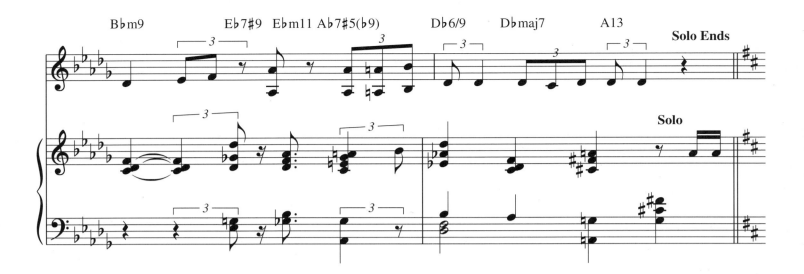

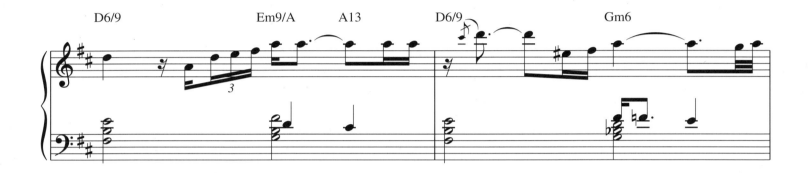

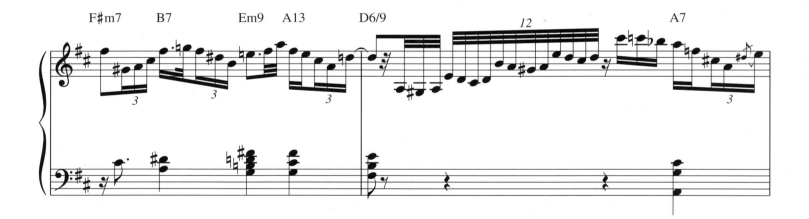

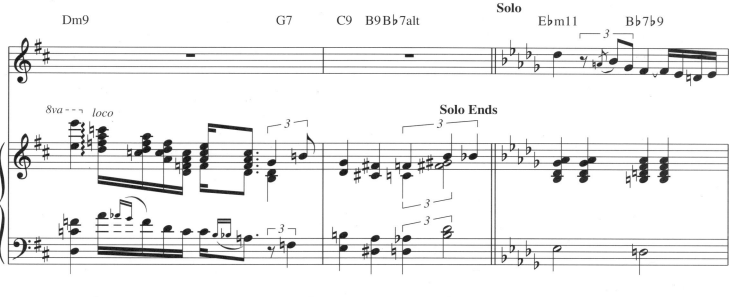

Solo

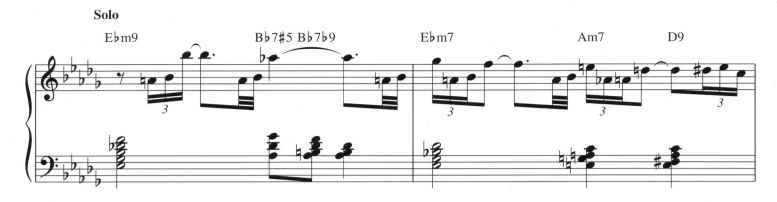

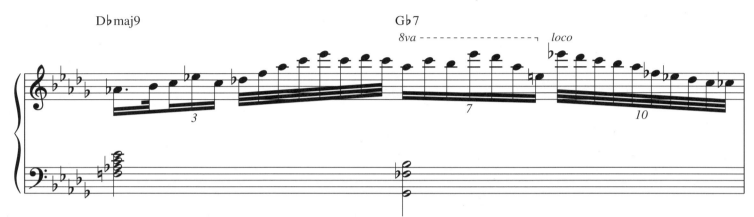

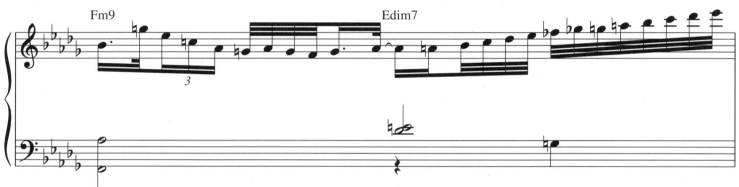

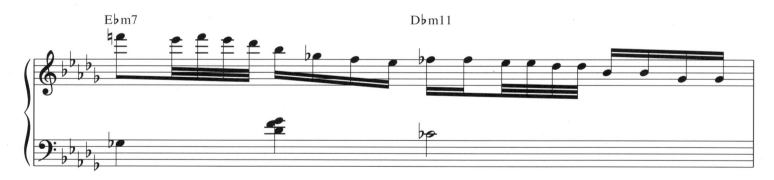

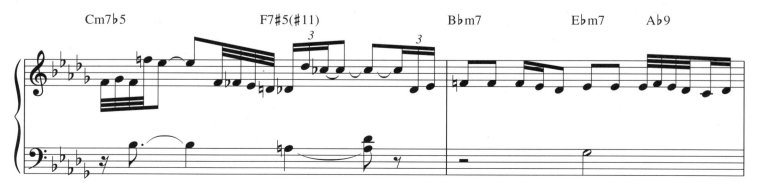

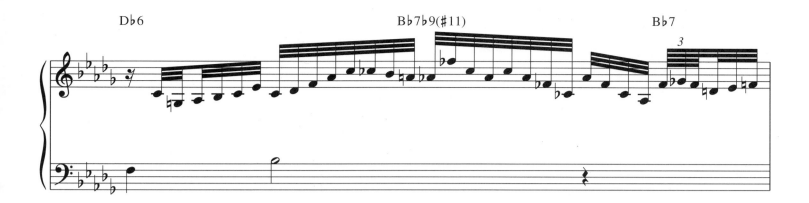

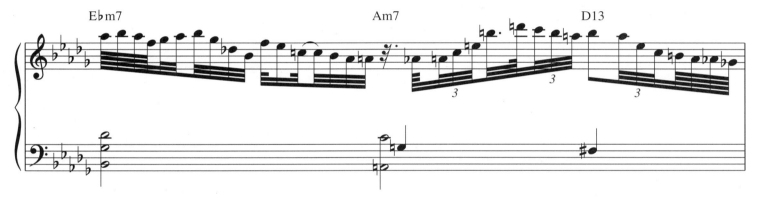

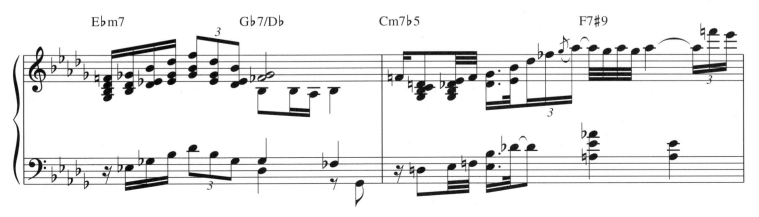

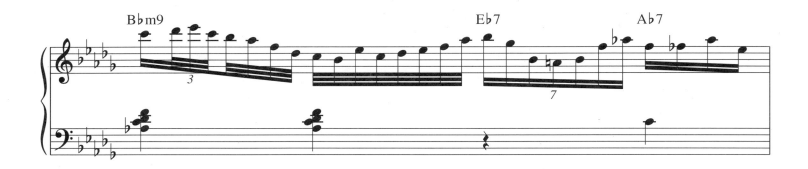

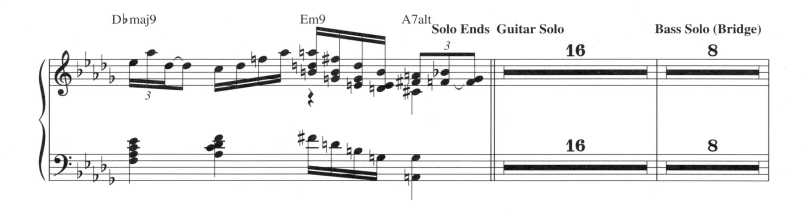

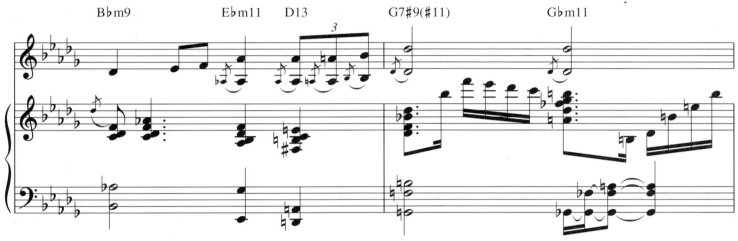

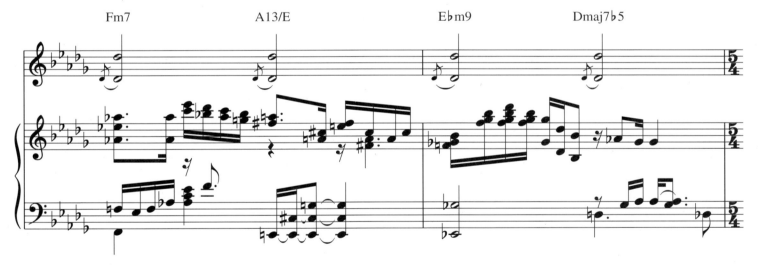

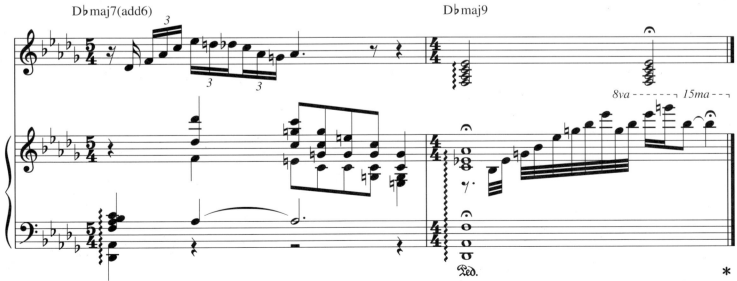

Caravan

from *SOPHISTICATED LADIES*

Words and Music by Duke Ellington, Irving Mills and Juan Tizol

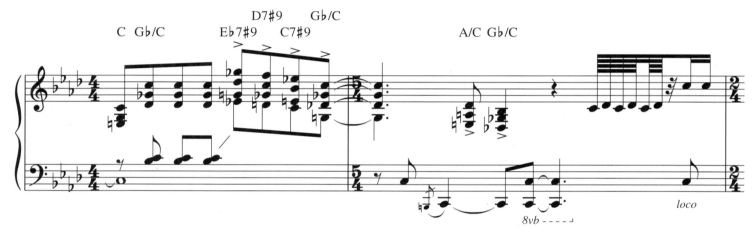

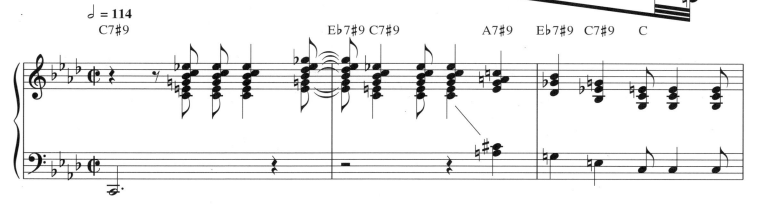

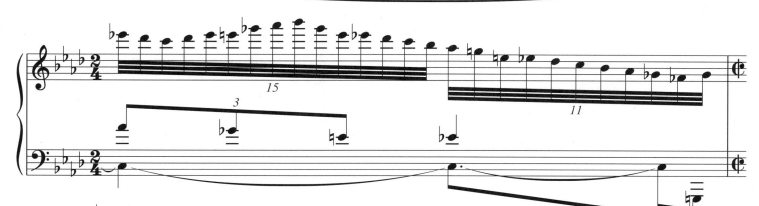

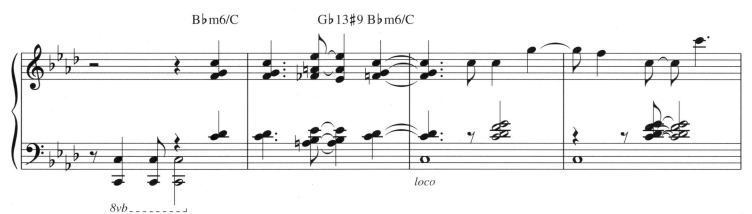

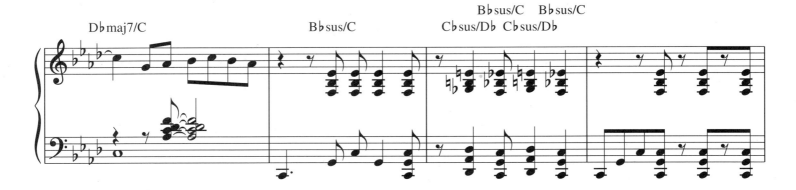

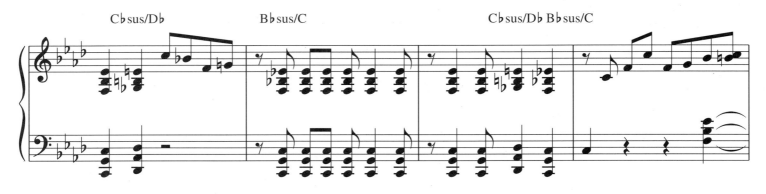

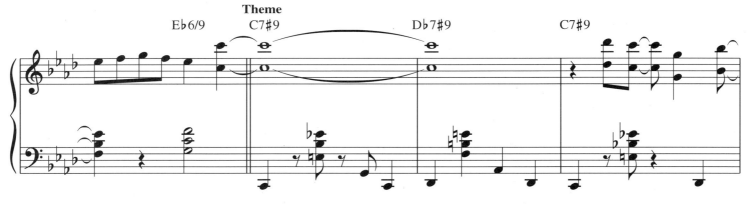

Theme

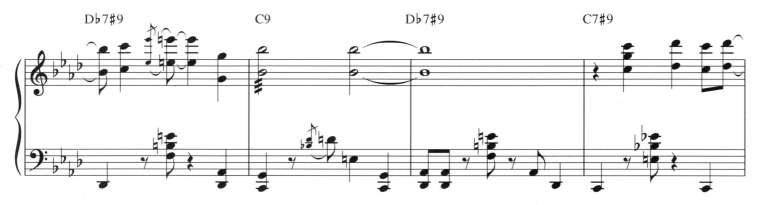

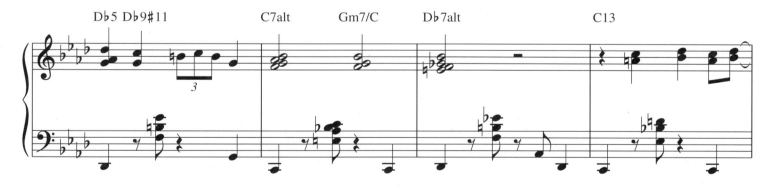

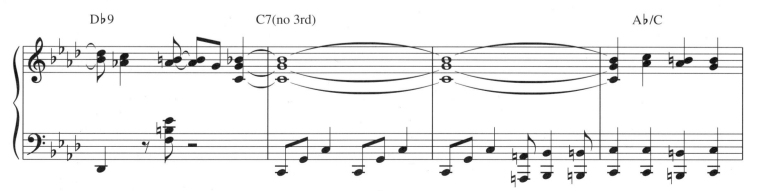

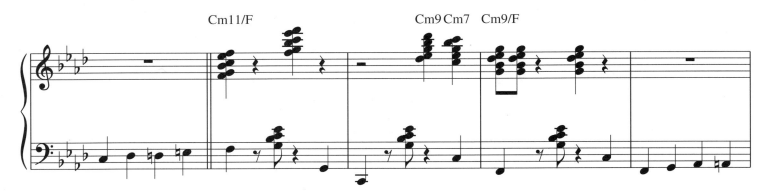

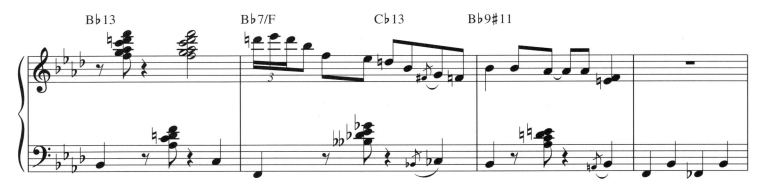

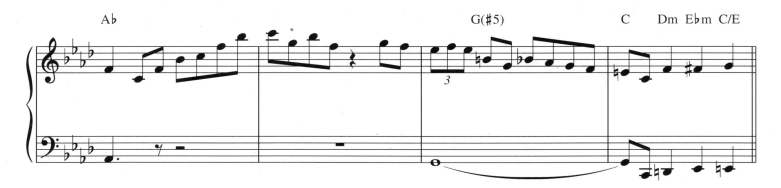

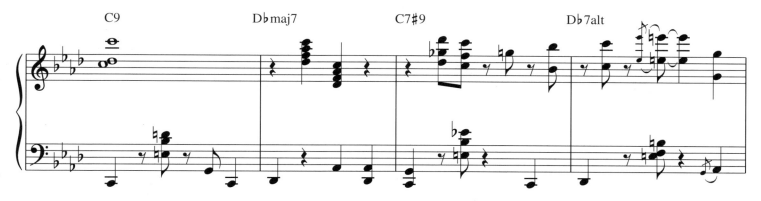

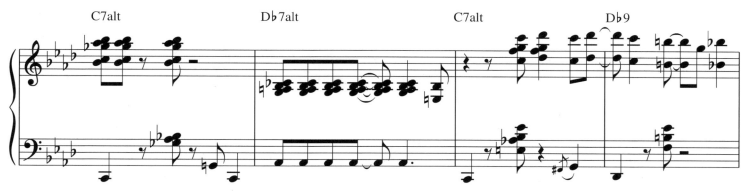

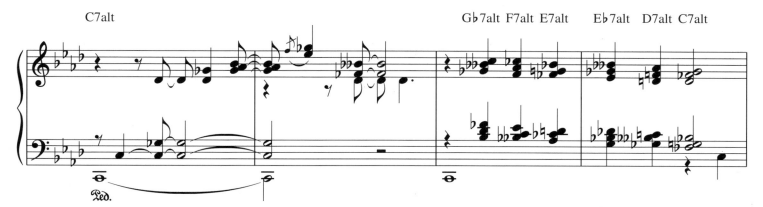

1st Chorus

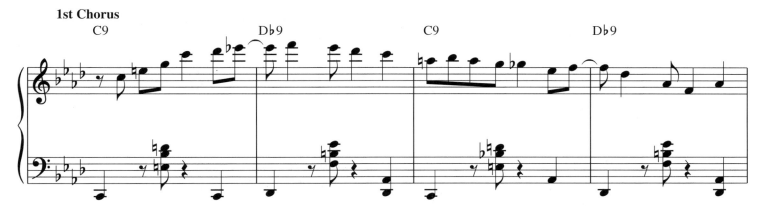

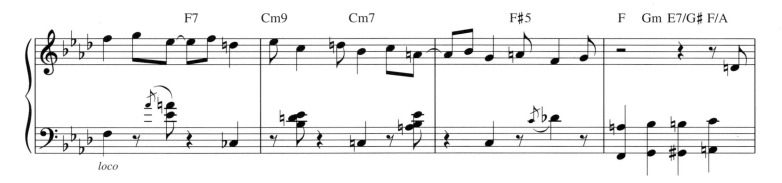

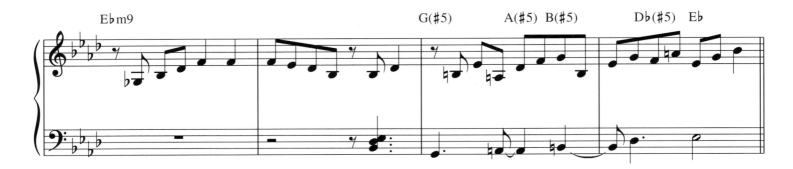

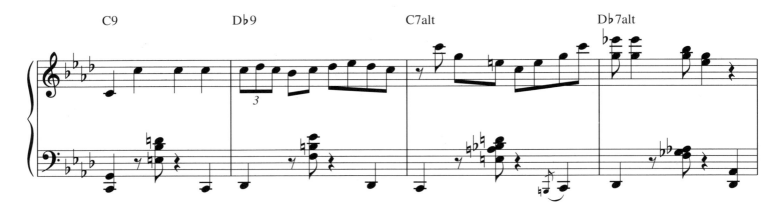

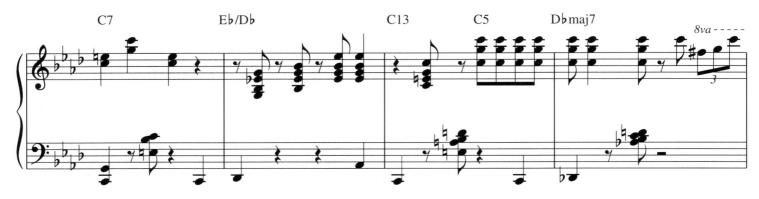

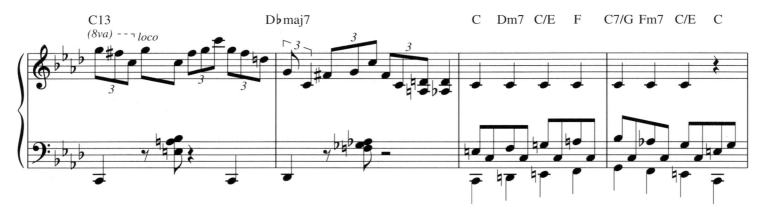

2nd Chorus

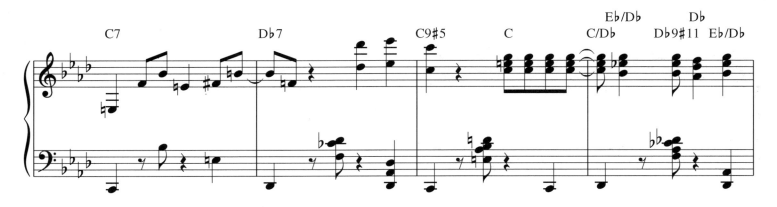

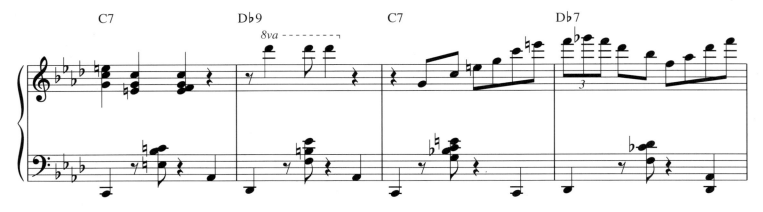

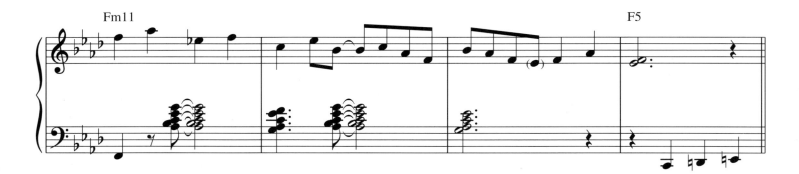

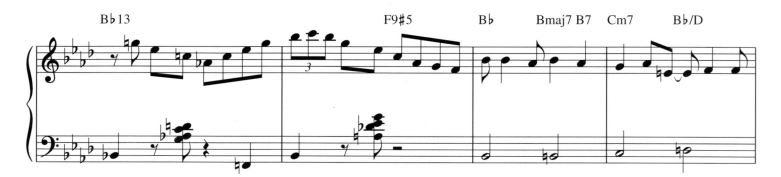

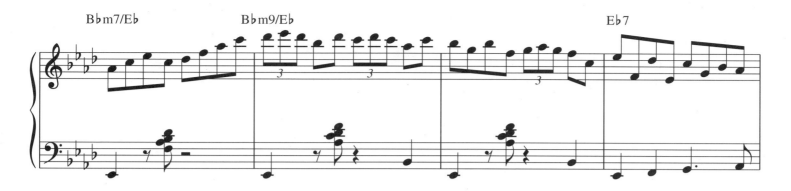

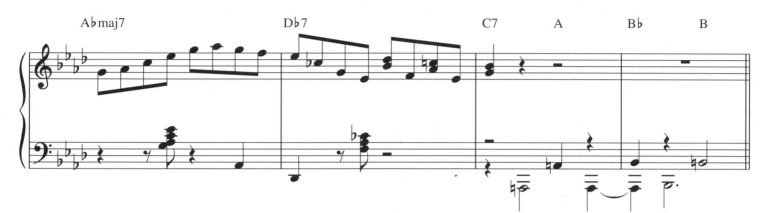

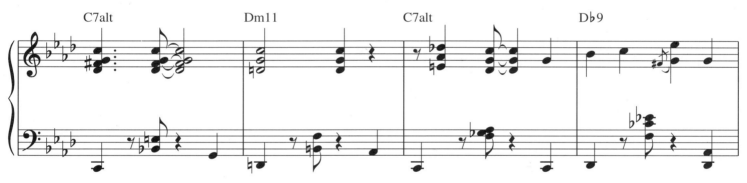

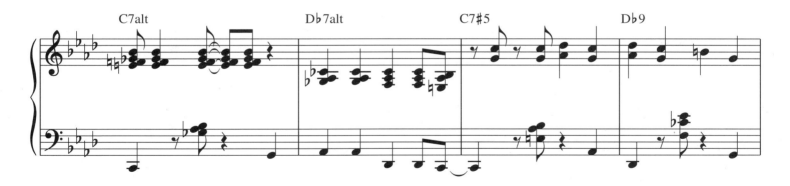

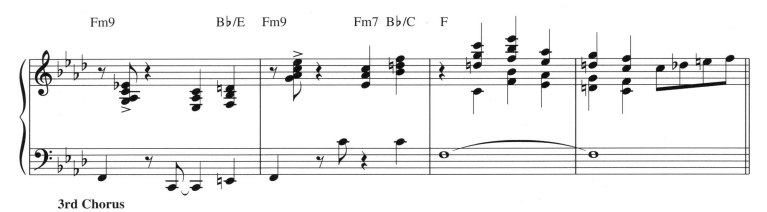

3rd Chorus

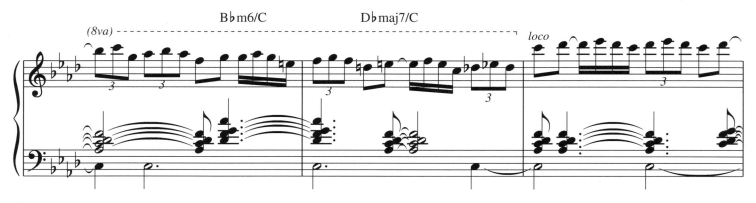

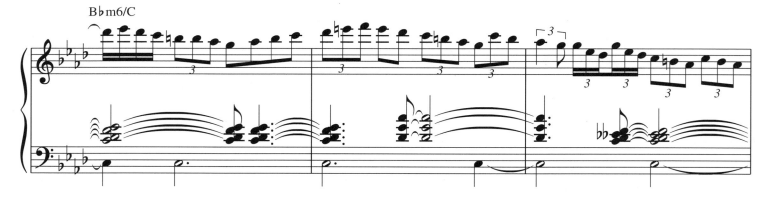

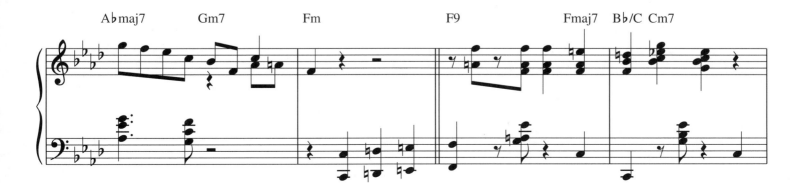

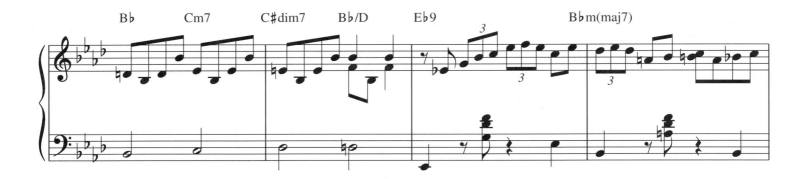

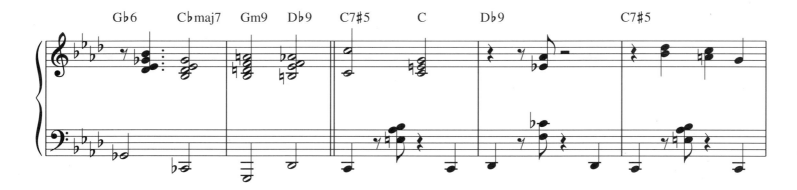

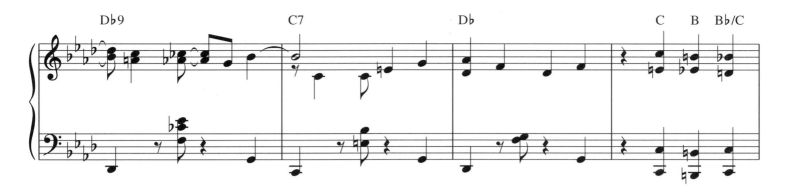

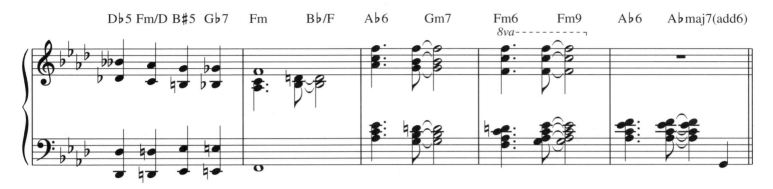

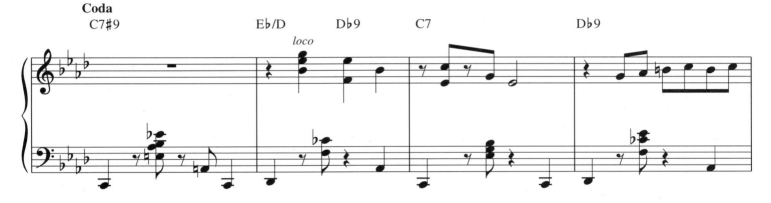

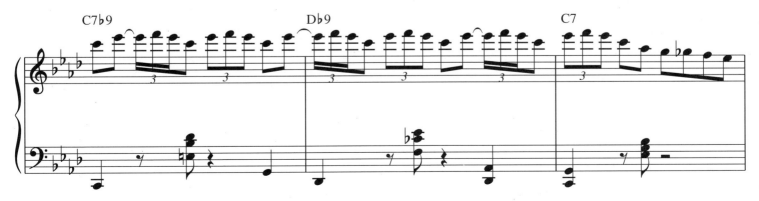

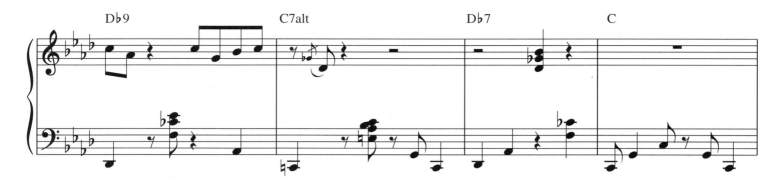

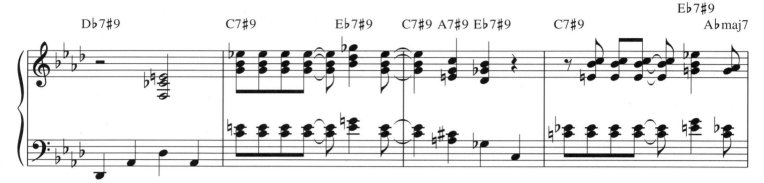

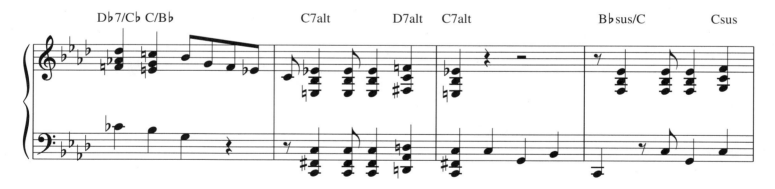

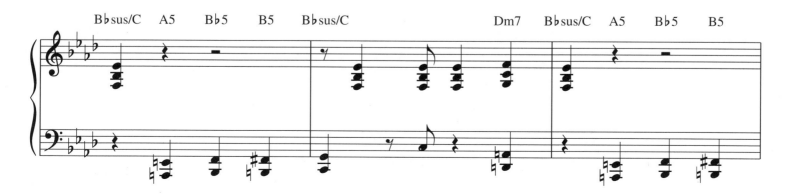

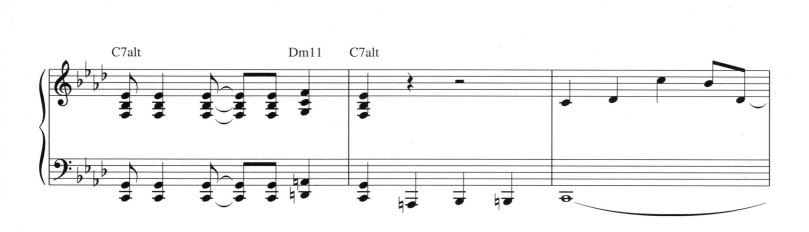

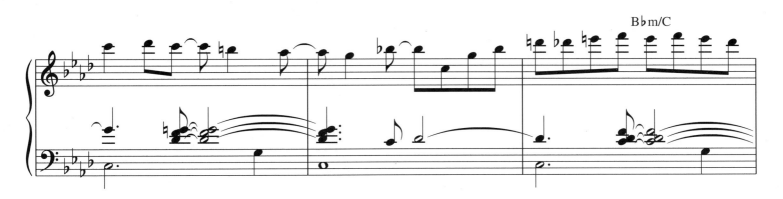

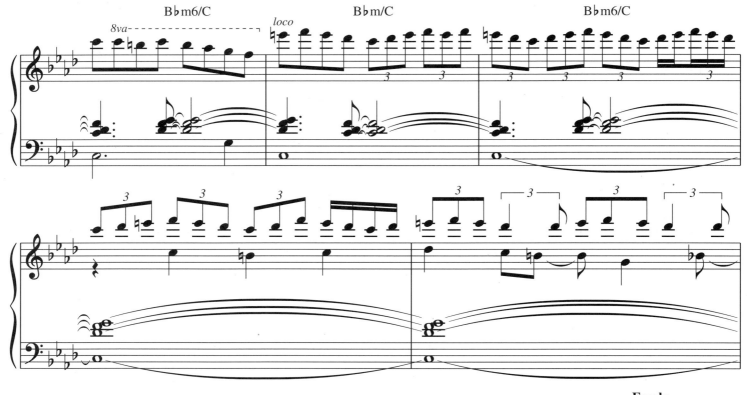

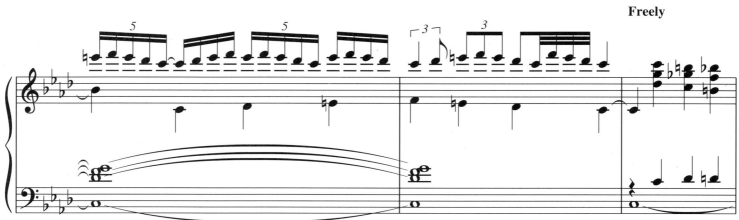

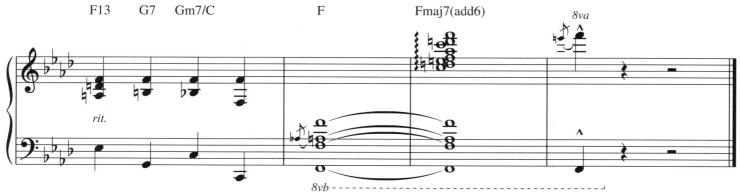

My One and Only Love

Words by Robert Mellin
Music by Guy Wood

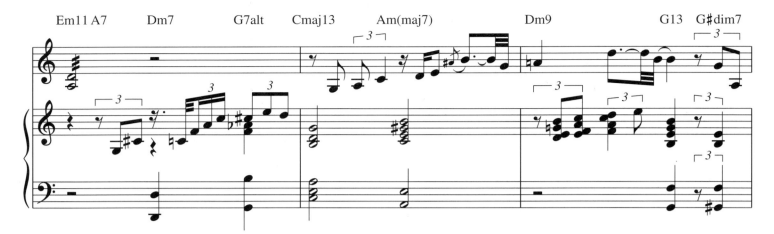

Em11 A7   Dm7   G7alt   Cmaj13   Am(maj7)   Dm9   G13   G#dim7

Am9   F6 Fmaj7 F6   Bm7♭5 E7#9 A7sus   A7 Dm7   G#dim7

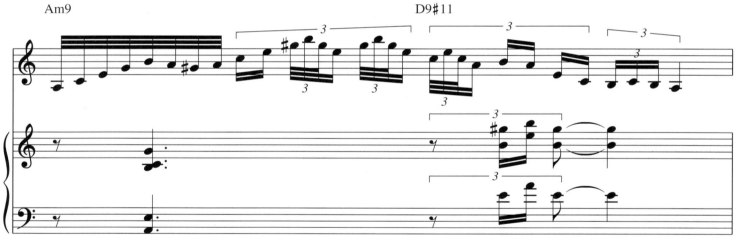

Am9   D9#11

Laid Back

Dm9   G13   C6/9   F#m7♭5   B7♭9

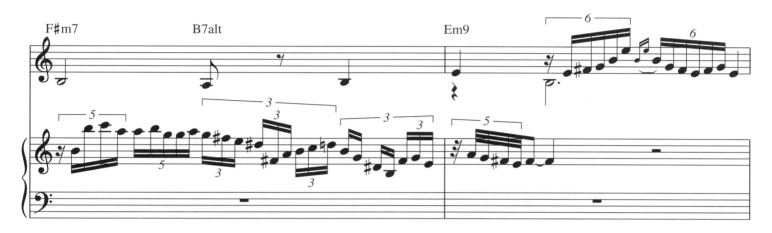

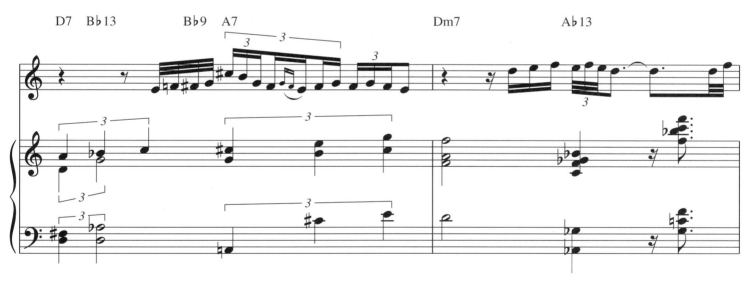

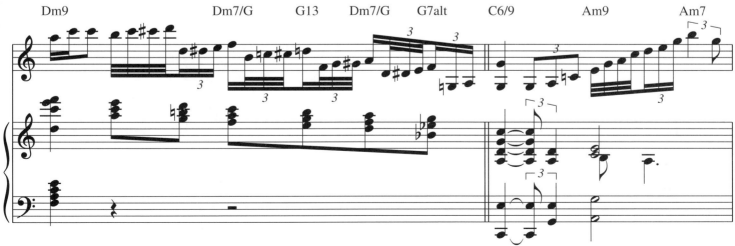

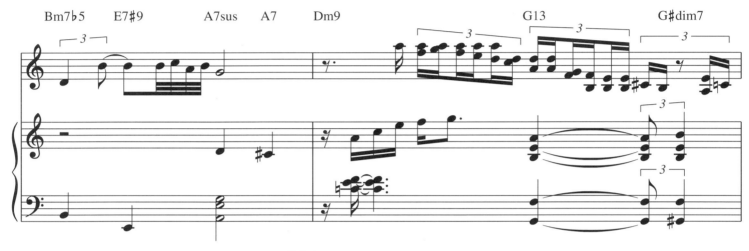

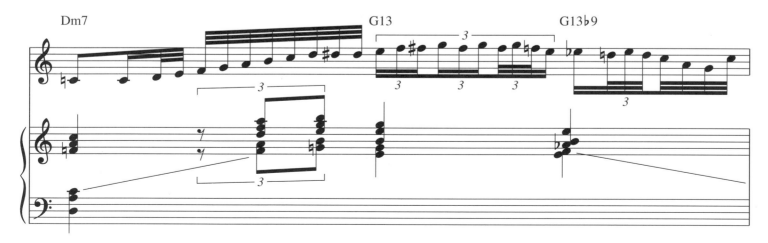

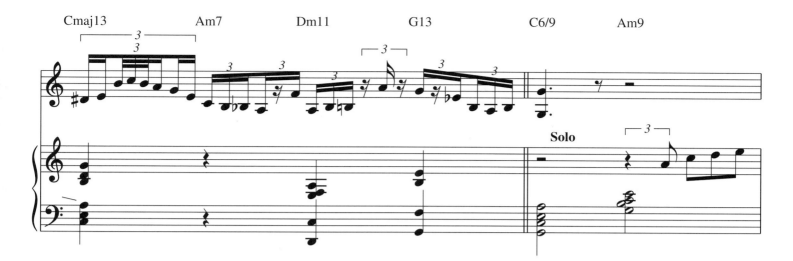

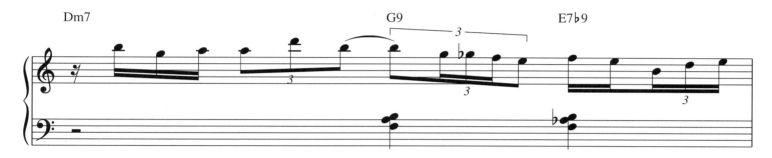

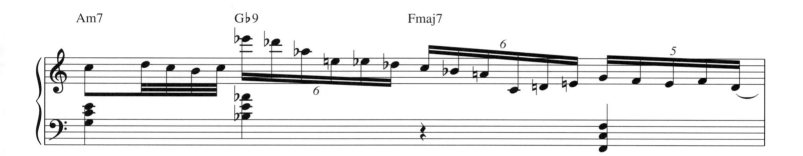

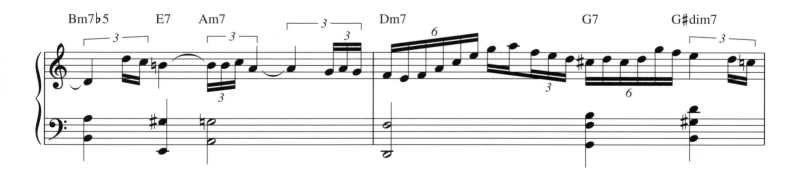

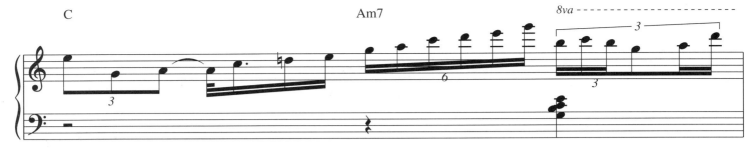

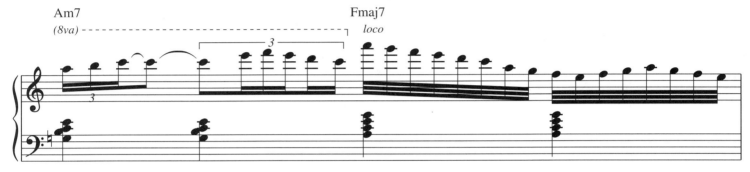

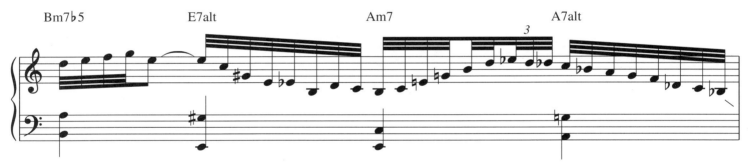

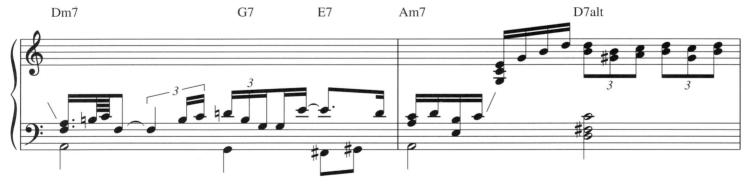

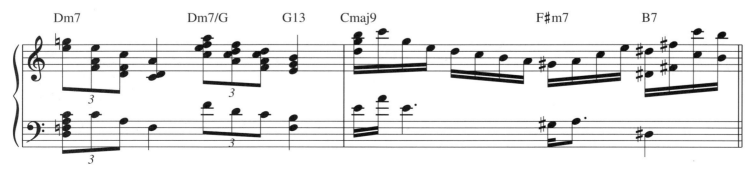

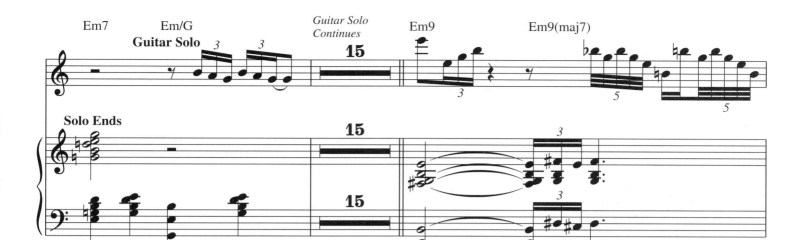

Laid Back

Freely

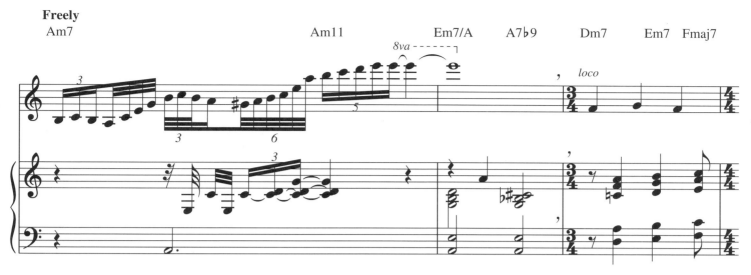

Cadenza

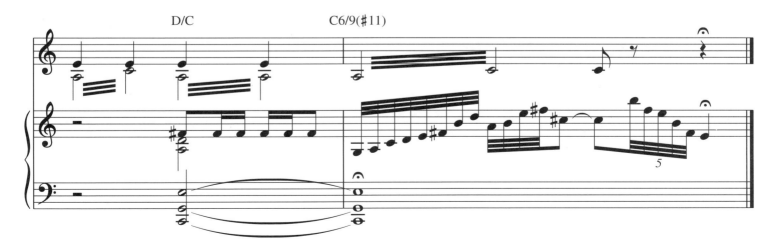

I Let a Song Go Out of My Heart

Words and Music by Duke Ellington, Henry Nemo, John Redmond and Irving Mills

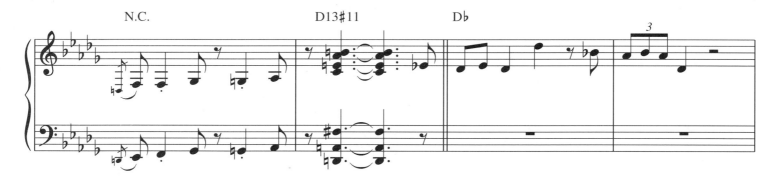

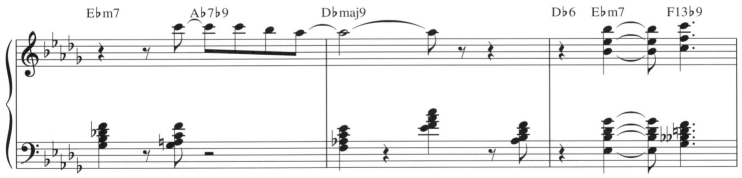

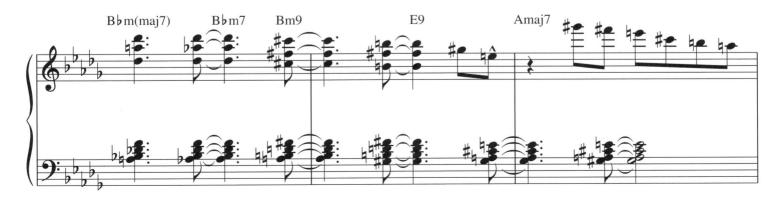

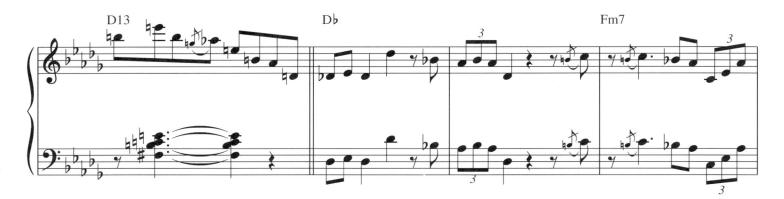

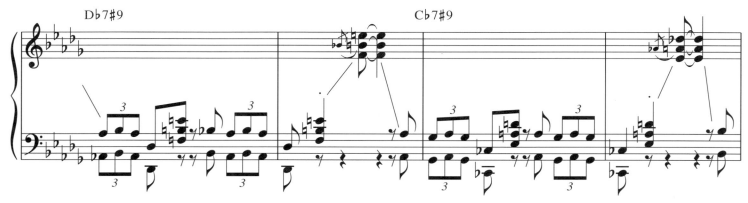

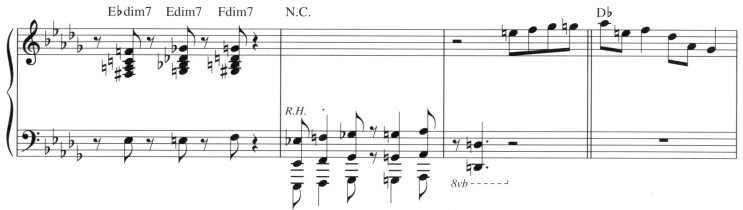

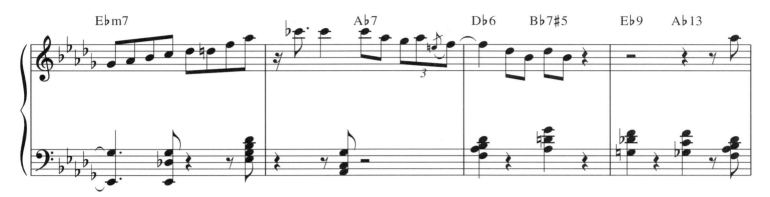

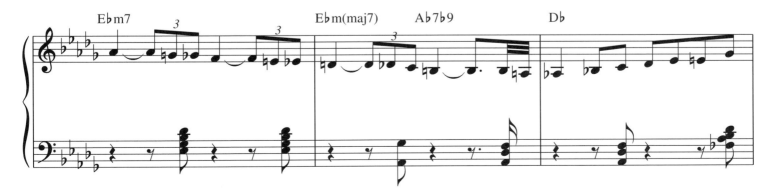

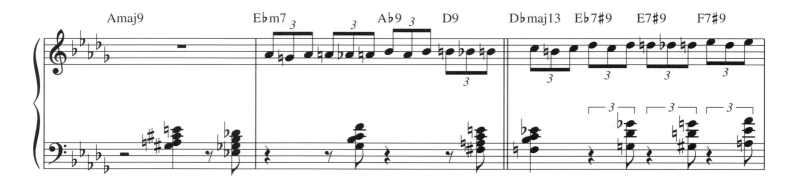

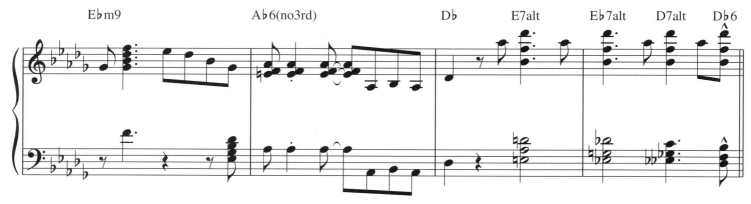

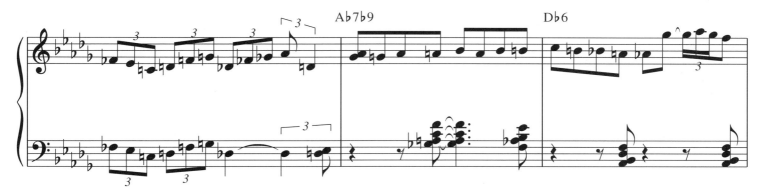

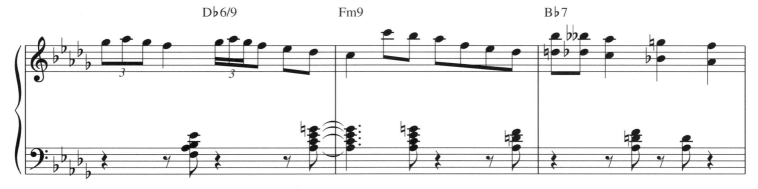

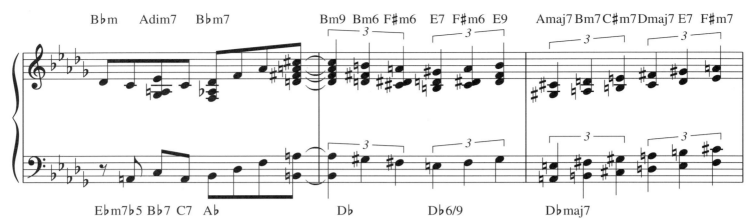

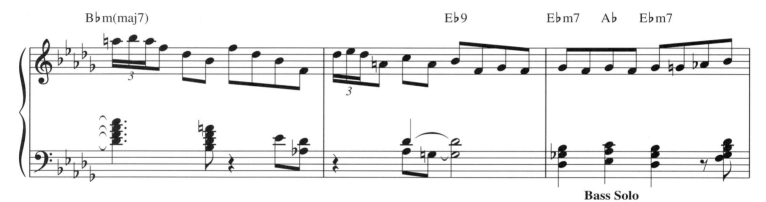

Bass Solo

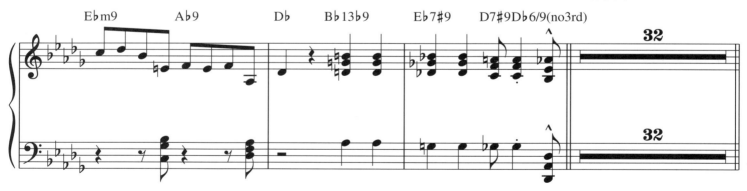

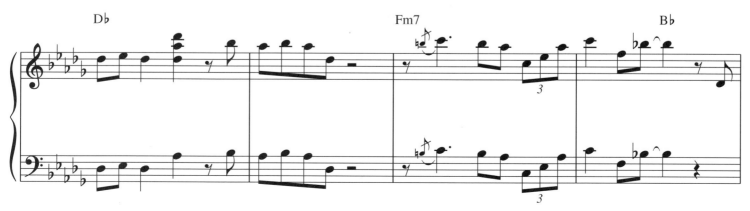

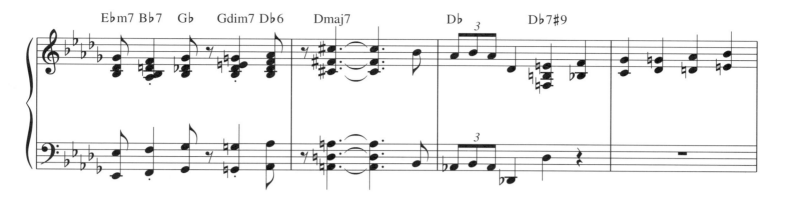

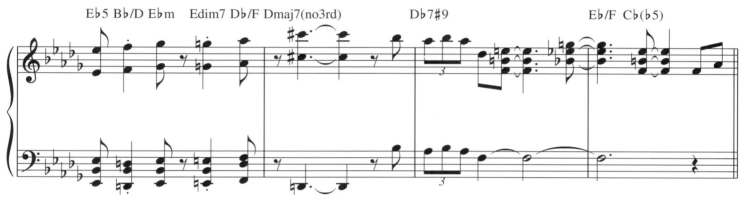

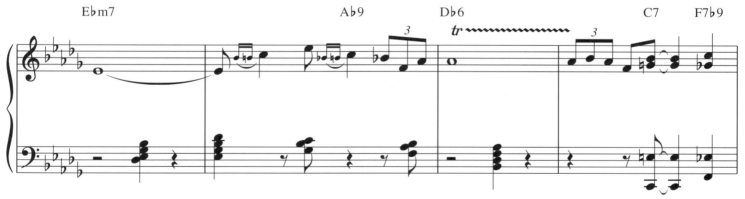

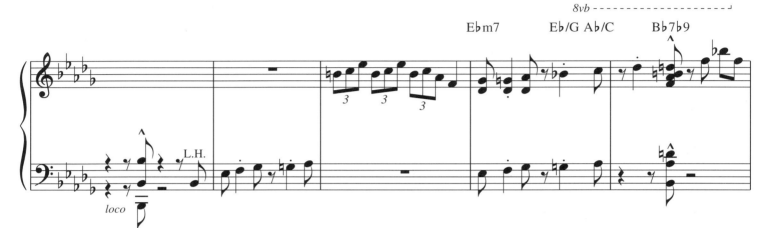

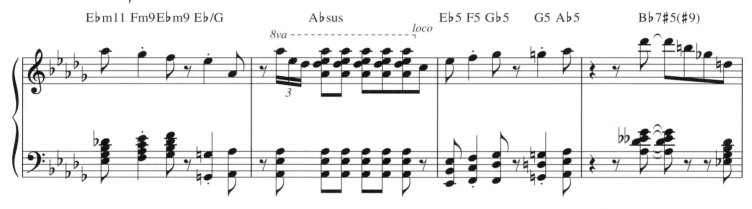

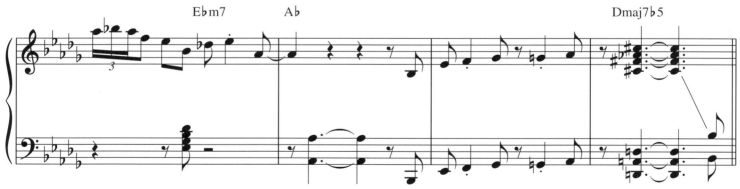

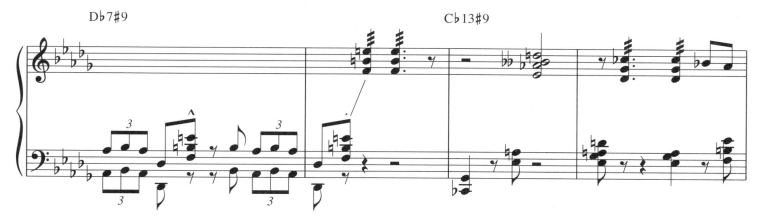

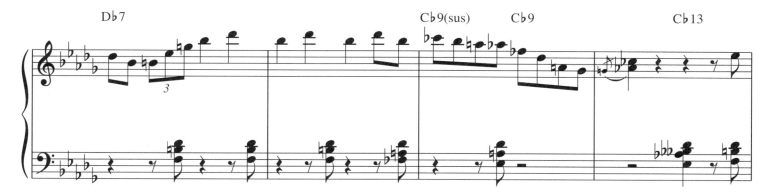

Recording Begins To Fade

etc.

It Might as Well Be Spring

from *STATE FAIR*

Lyrics by Oscar Hammerstein II
Music by Richard Rodgers

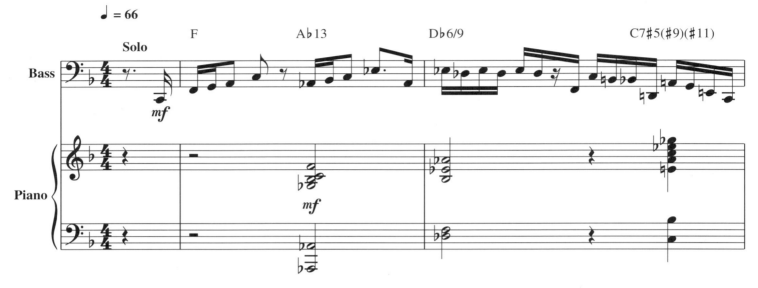

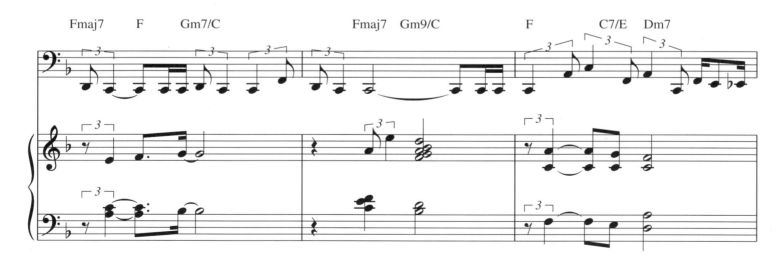

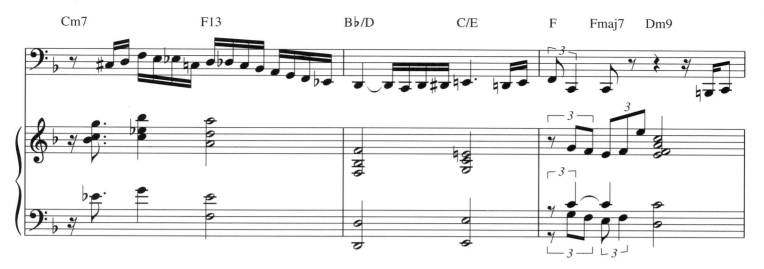

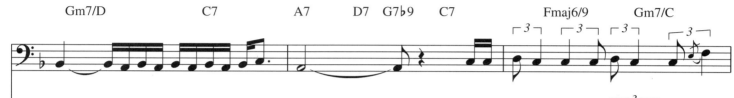

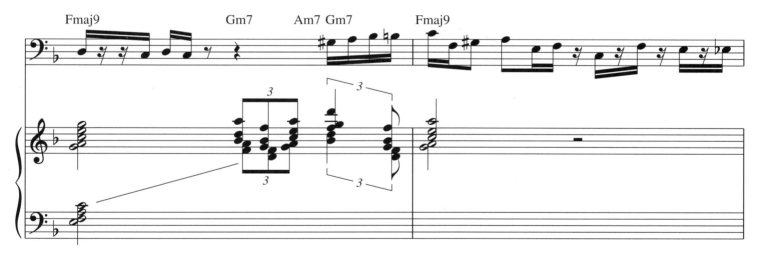

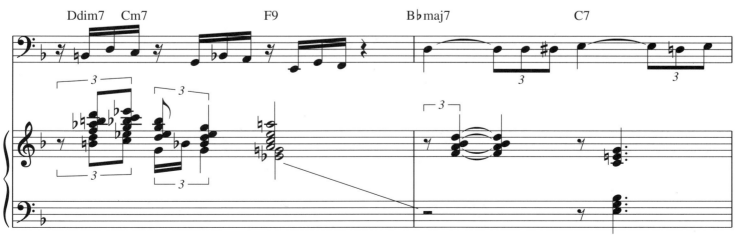

52

Guitar Solo Ends

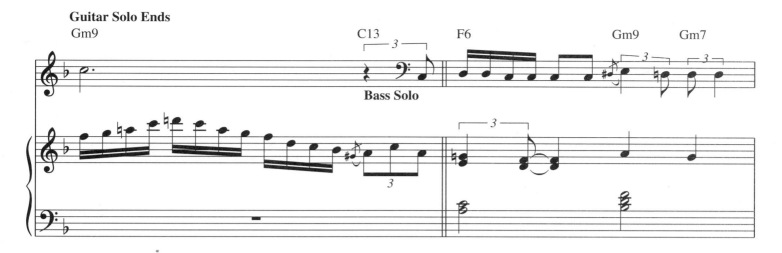

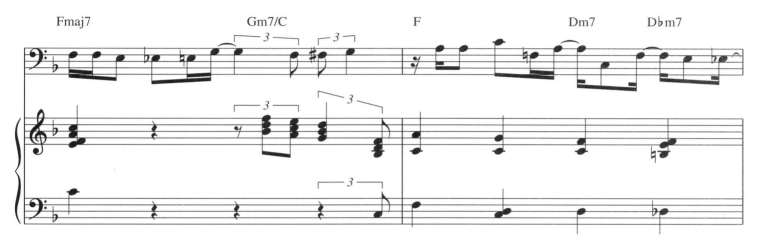

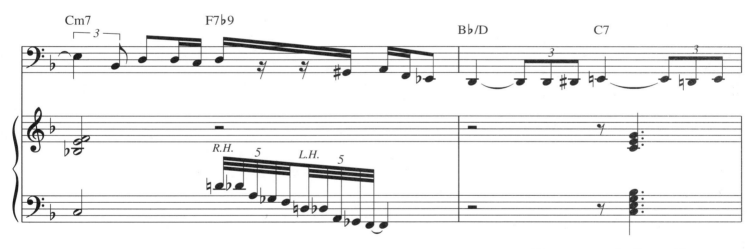

53

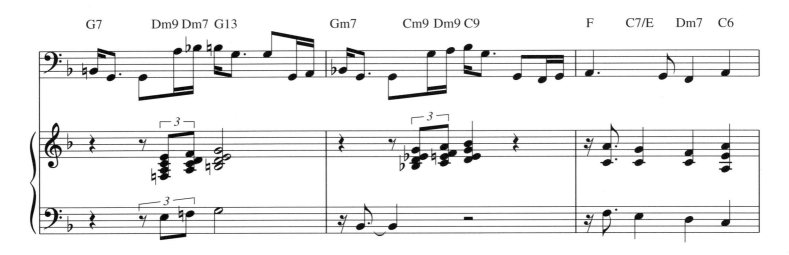

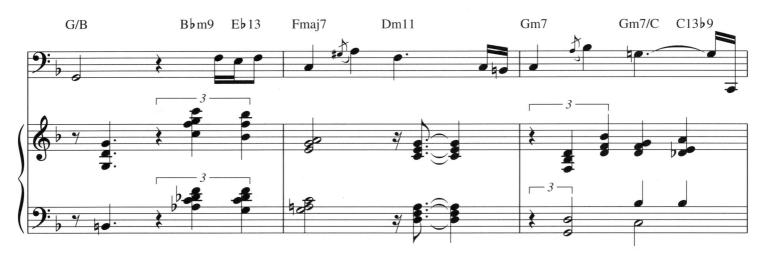

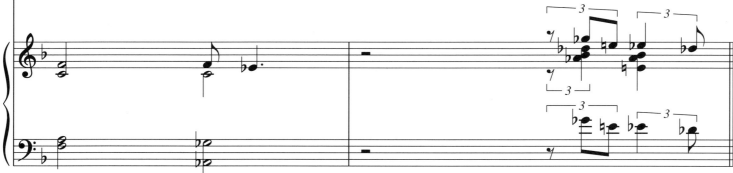

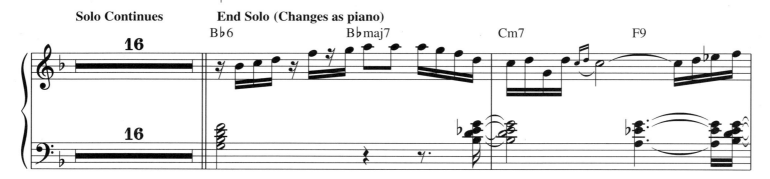

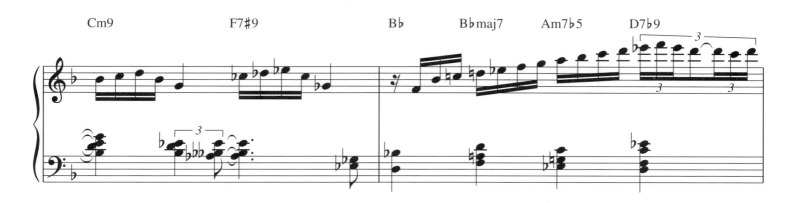

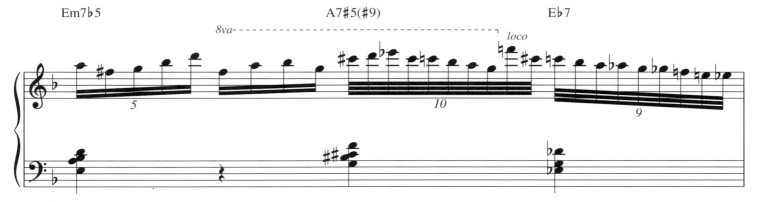

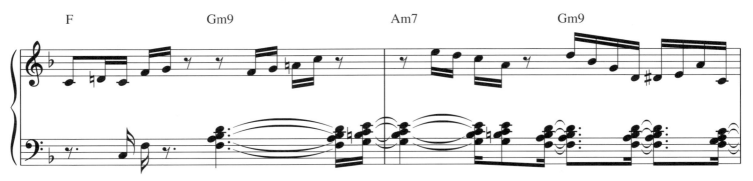

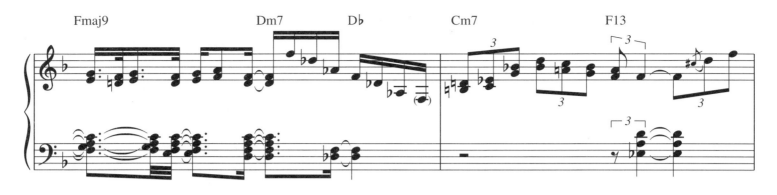

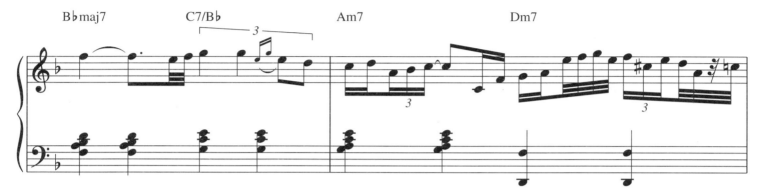

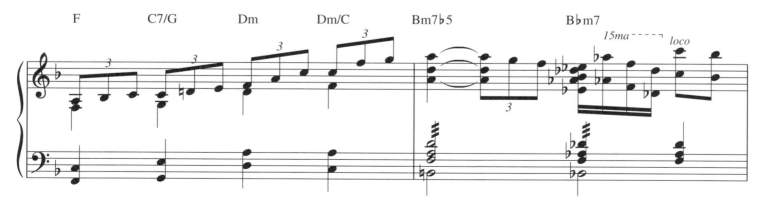

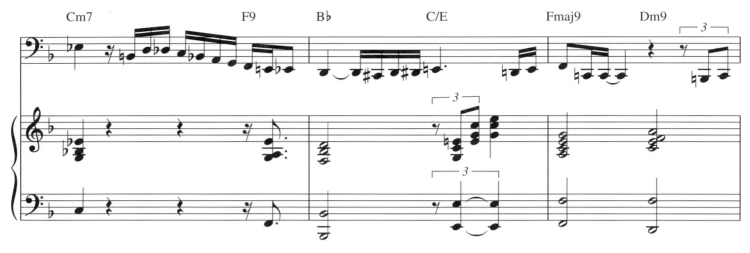

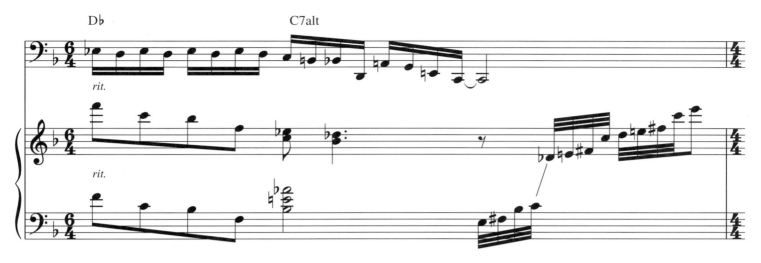

Freely (Cadenza)

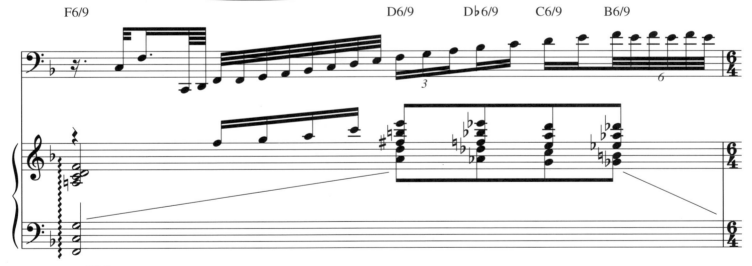

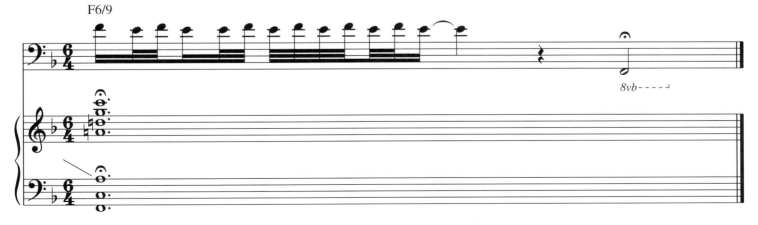

Small Fry

from the Paramount Motion Picture *SING, YOU SINNERS*

Words by Frank Loesser
Music by Hoagy Carmichael

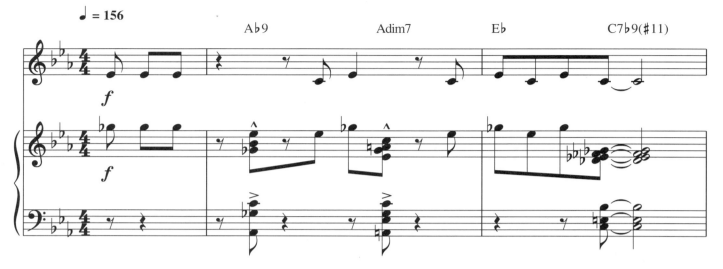

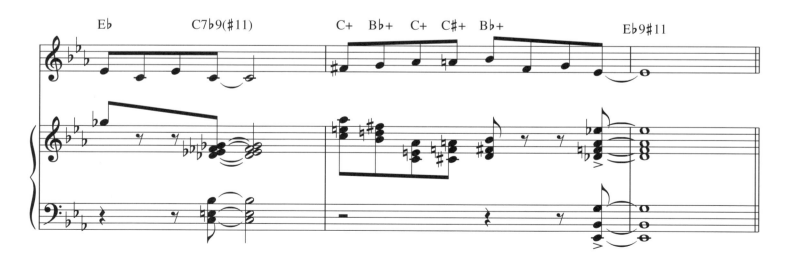

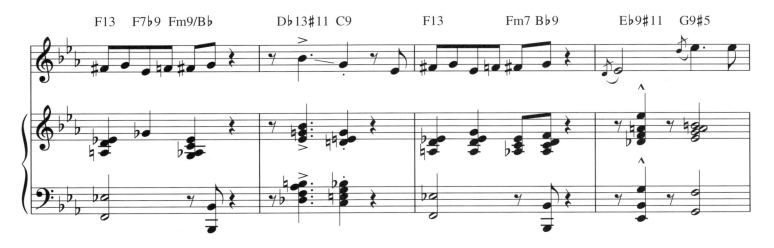

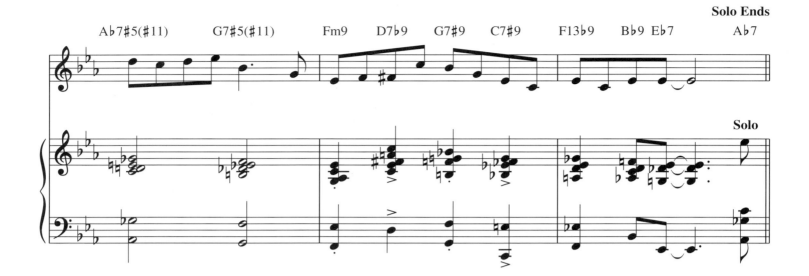

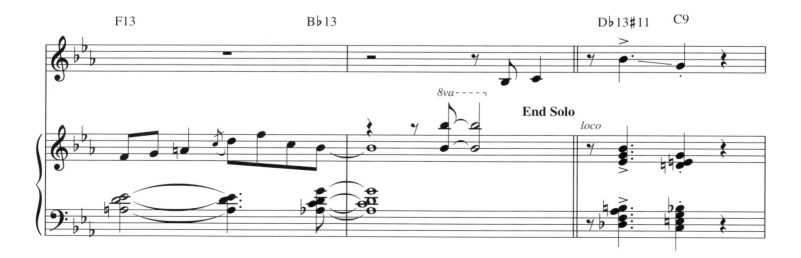

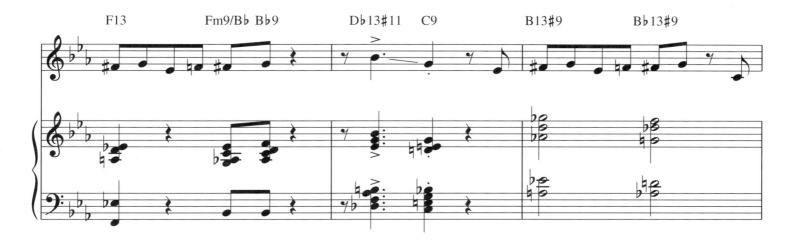

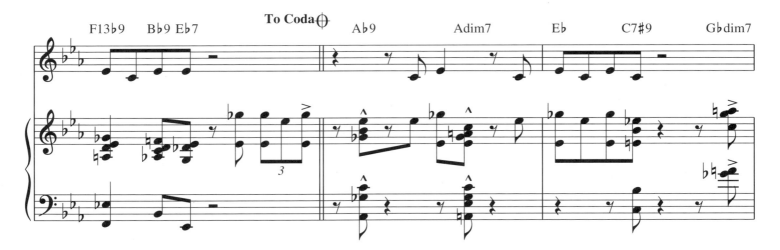

Guitar Solo

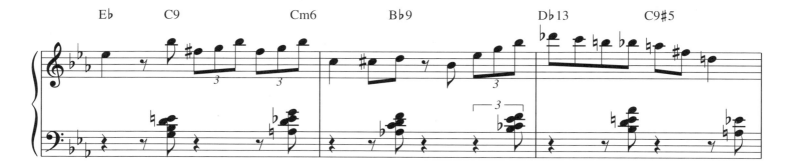

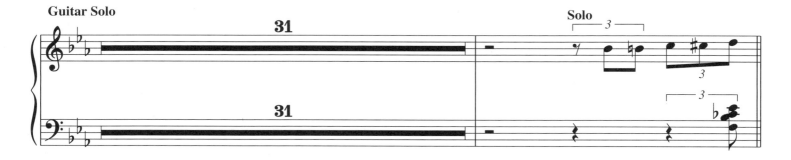

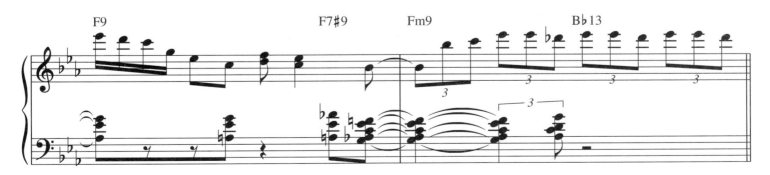

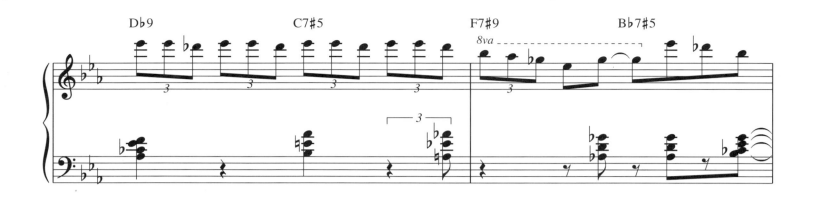

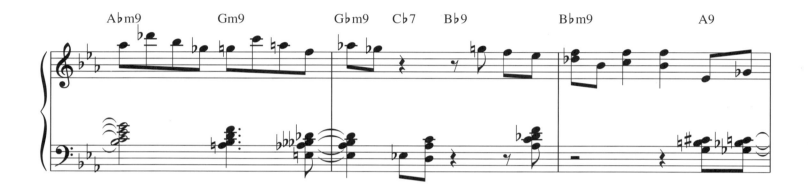

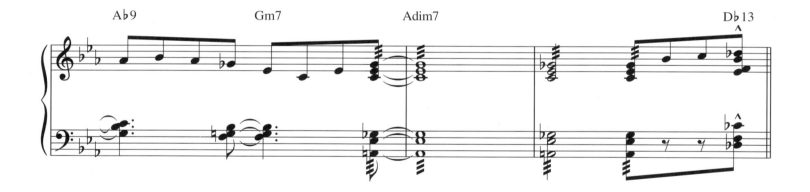

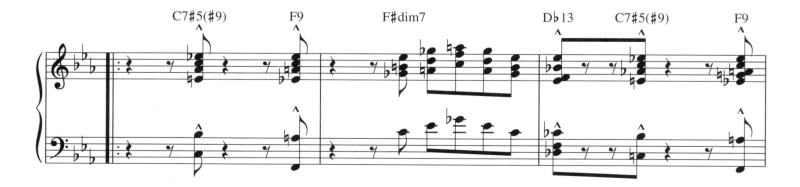

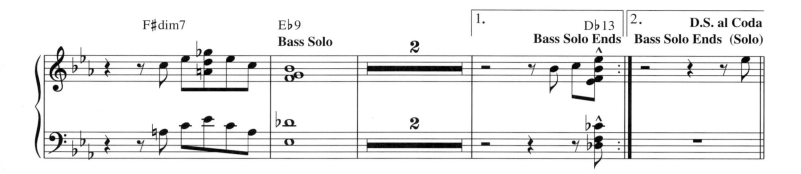

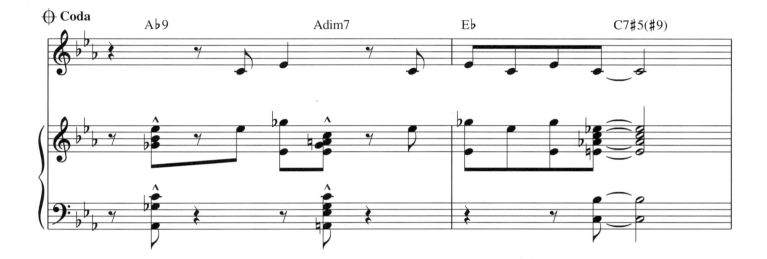

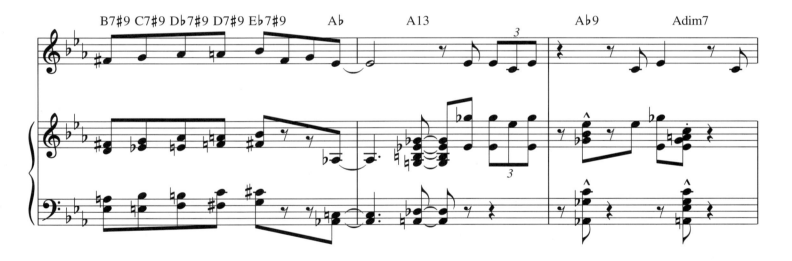

Where Is Love?

from the Columbia Pictures - Romulus Film *OLIVER!*

Words and Music by Lionel Bart

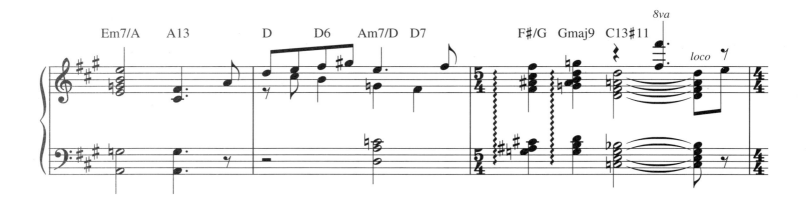

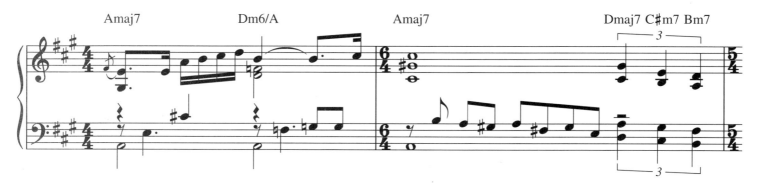

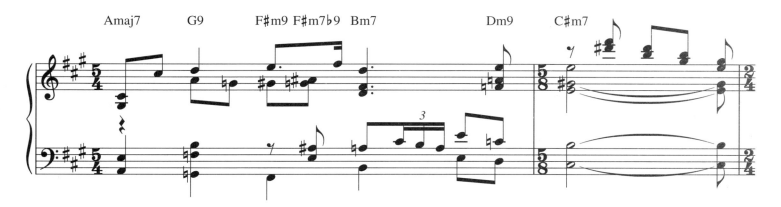

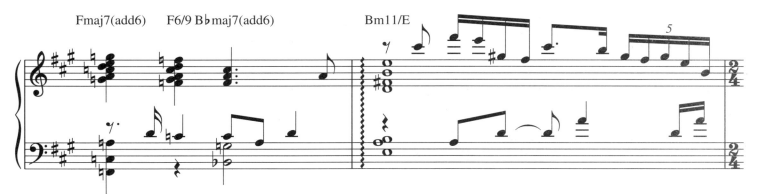

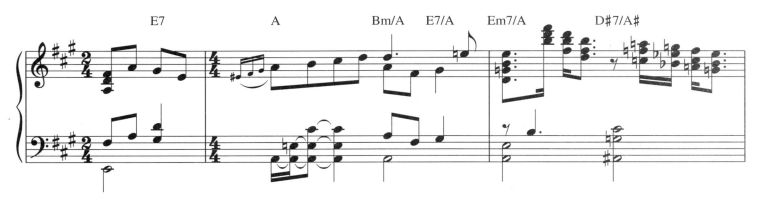

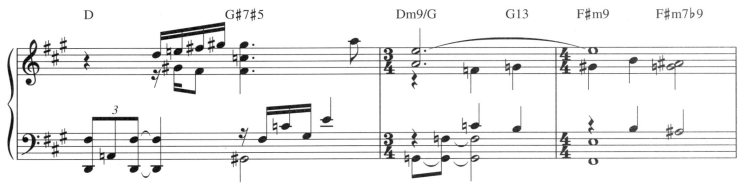

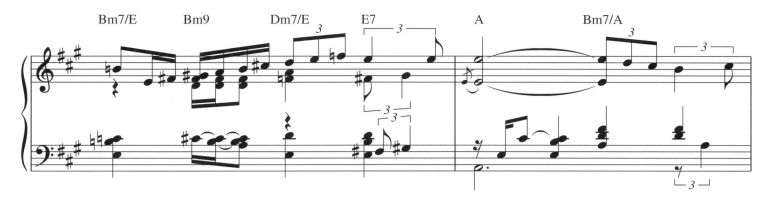

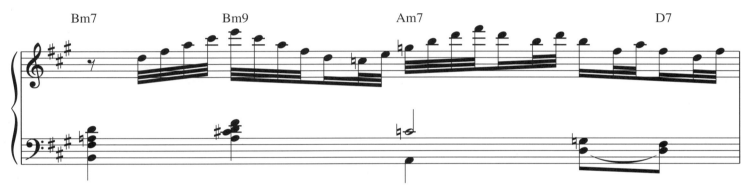

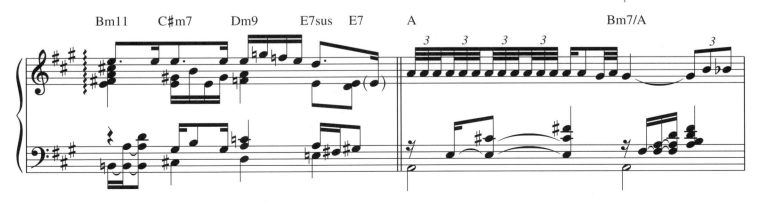

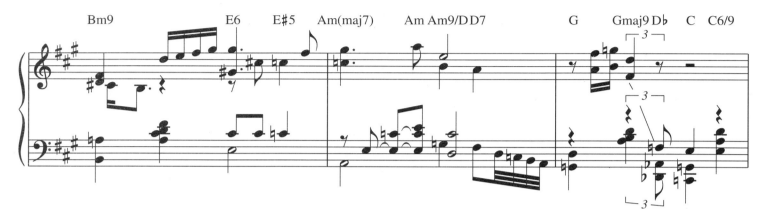

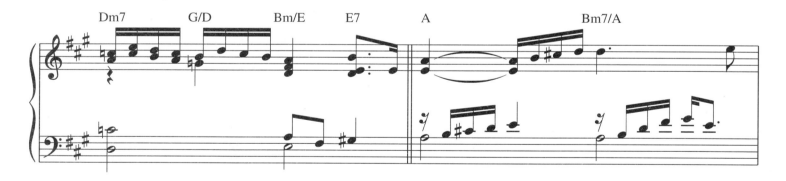

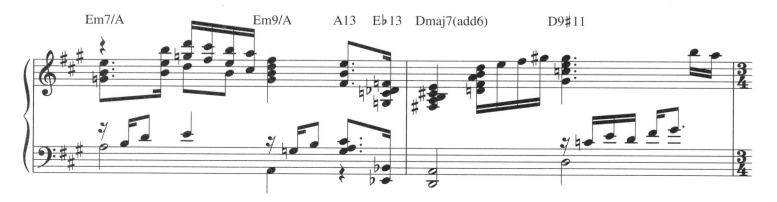

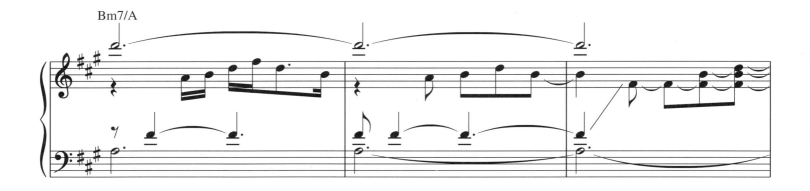

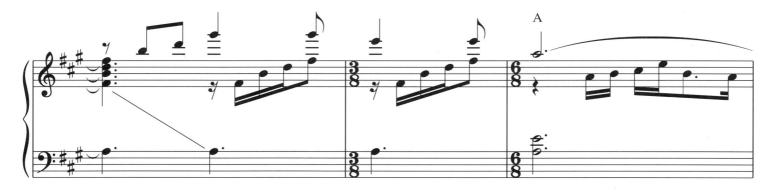

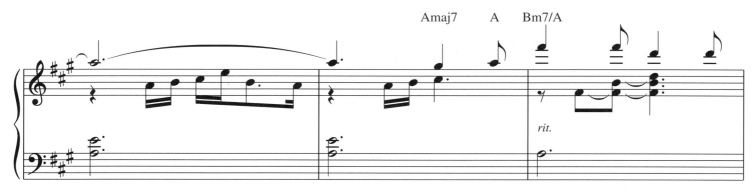

You Call It Madness

(But I Call It Love)

Words and Music by Con Conrad, Gladys DuBois, Russ Columbo and Paul Gregory

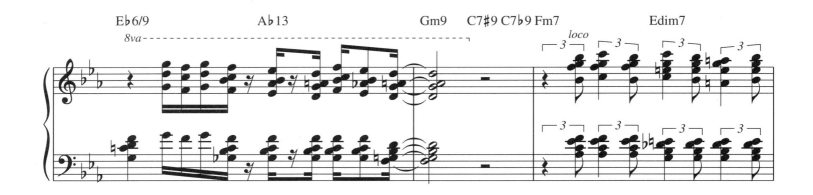

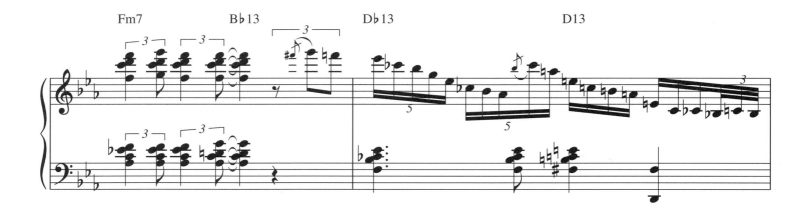

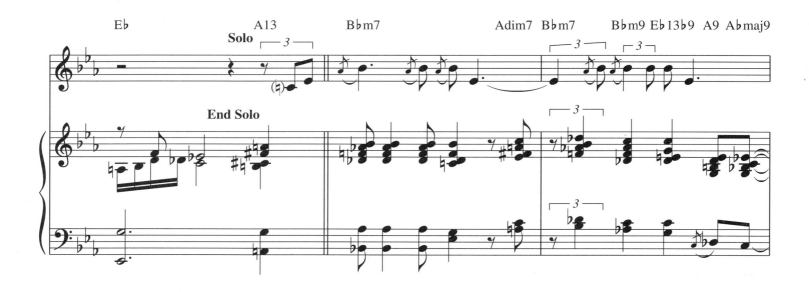

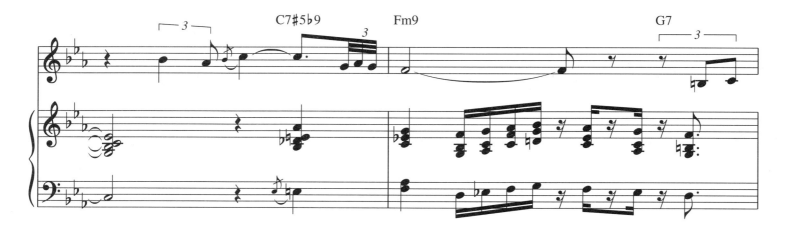

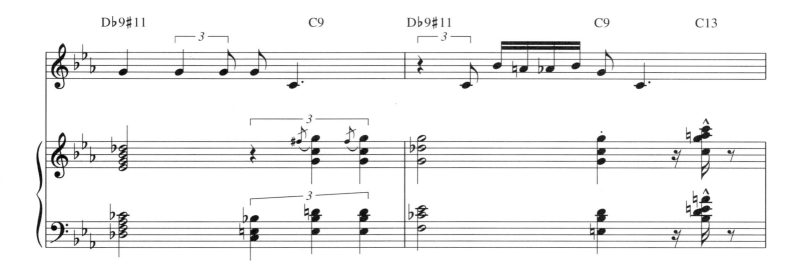

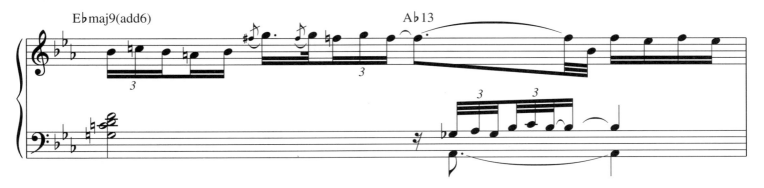

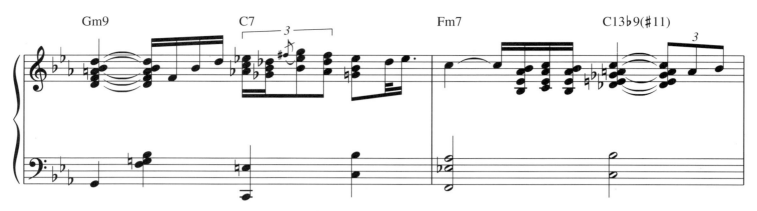

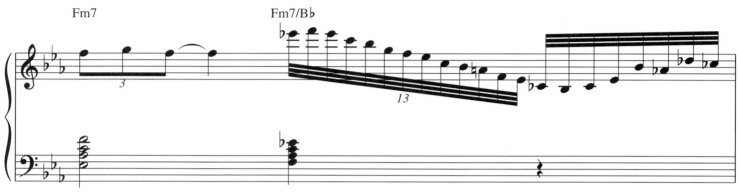

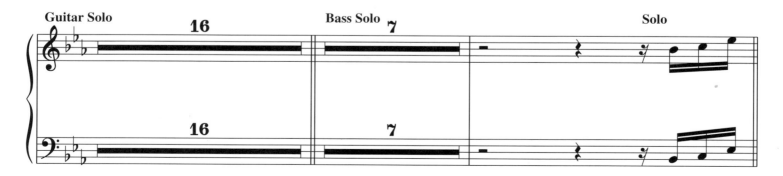

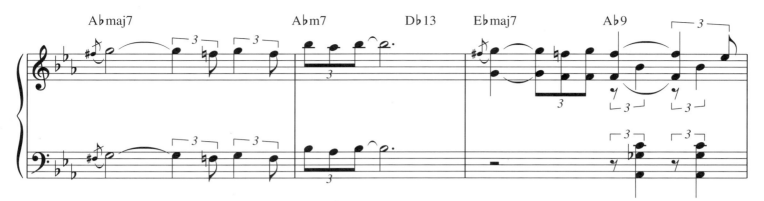

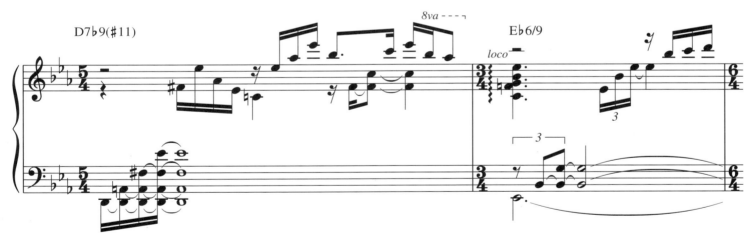

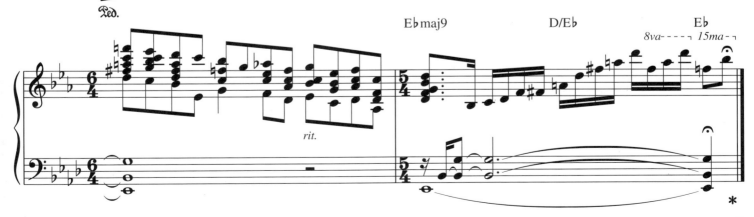

DISCOGRAPHY

All recordings on the Concord Jazz label except as noted.

BODY AND SOUL, SMALL FRY – LP: CJ-193; CD: CCD-4193

CARAVAN, I LET A SONG GO OUT OF MY HEART – LP + CD: MPS/Verve 821 151

IT MIGHT AS WELL BE SPRING – LP: CJ-338; CD: CCD-4338

MY ONE AND ONLY LOVE – LP: CJ-394; CD: CCD-4394

WHERE IS LOVE? – CD: CCD-4658

YOU CALL IT MADNESS (BUT I CALL IT LOVE) – LP: CJ-136; CD: CCD-4136